www.heinemann.co.uk/library
Visit our website to find out more information about Heinemann Library books.

To order:
☎ Phone 44 (0) 1865 888066

🗎 Send a fax to 44 (0) 1865 314091

💻 Visit the Heinemann Bookshop at www.heinemann.co.uk/library to browse our catalogue and order online.

Heinemann Library is an imprint of Pearson Education Limited, a company incorporated in England and Wales having its registered office at Edinburgh Gate, Harlow, Essex, CM20 2JE – Registered company number: 00872828

Heinemann is a registered trademark of Pearson Education Ltd.
Text © Pearson Education Limited 2008
First published in hardback in 2008
Paperback edition first published in 2009
The moral rights of the proprietor have been asserted.

Edited by Sarah Shannon, Catherine Clarke, and Laura Knowles
Designed by Joanna Hinton-Malivoire, Victoria Bevan, and Hart McLeod
Picture research by Liz Alexander and Rebecca Sodergren
Production by Duncan Gilbert
Originated by Chroma Graphics (Overseas) Pte. Ltd
Printed and bound in China by Leo Paper Group

ISBN 978 0 431932 84 2 (hardback)
12 11 10 09 08
10 9 8 7 6 5 4 3 2 1
ISBN 978 0 431933 03 0 (paperback)
13 12 11 10 09
10 9 8 7 6 5 4 3 2 1

British Library Cataloguing in Publication Data
Barraclough, Sue
   Earth's resources. - (Investigate)
   333.7

A full catalogue record for this book is available from the British Library.

Acknowledgements
©Alamy pp. **10** (Rolf Richardson), **16** (Paul Felix Photography); ©Corbis pp. **6**, **30** (Scott Barrow/Solus-Veer), **15** (Virgo Productions/zefa), **20** (Philippe Renault/Hemis); ©Getty pp. **5** (Mark Kelley), **8** (Rachel Weill); ©Getty Images pp. **12** (Steven Wooster), **13** (Peter Ridge), **17**, **23**, **24**, **30** (PhotoDisc), **25** (BAVARIA), **7**, **30**; © 2008 Jupiter Images Corporation p. **26**; ©NASA p. **4**; ©PhotoDisc pp. **23**, **24**; ©Photolibrary p. **11**, **30** (Lester Lefkowitz), **22** (Paul Nevin), **27** (Danièle Schneider/Photononstop); ©PunchStock p. **29** (Digital Vision); ©Reuters p. **14**; ©Rex Features p. **18**, **30** (Image Source); ©Science Photo Library pp. **19**, **28** (Martin Bond), **21** (Richard Folwell).

Cover photograph of logging in forest reproduced with permission of ©Corbis (moodboard).

Every effort has been made to contact copyright holders of material reproduced in this book. Any omissions will be rectified in subsequent printings if notice is given to the publishers.

Contents

Some words are shown in bold, **like this**. You can find out what they mean by looking in the glossary.

Earth's resources

Earth's resources are the things we get from Earth.
The most important resources are air, water, and soil.
We need these things to stay alive.

We need:
➠ air to breathe
➠ water to drink
➠ soil to grow food.

Other resources that we use are **materials** and **fuels**. Materials are things we can use to make things. Clay, rocks, and metal are materials. Fuels are things that can be burned to make light and heat. Wood and **coal** are fuels.

Wood is used as a fuel and to make things. ➔

Air and water

All living things need air and water to stay alive. You cannot see air, but it is all around you. You can feel air when it is windy. All living things need clean air to stay alive.

Water covers most of Earth. Oceans and seas are salt water. You cannot drink salt water. Rivers and lakes are fresh water. You can drink fresh water. Only a very small amount of water on Earth is fresh water.

Water falls from the clouds as rain and makes puddles.

Q Why do people need water?

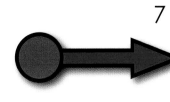

People need to drink water to stay alive and healthy.

We use water to:

➡ wash ourselves and our clothes

➡ cook food

➡ water plants.

8

Water is important so you should not waste it.
You can save water if you:

➜ turn off the tap as you brush your teeth

➜ take a shower instead of a bath

➜ ask an adult to mend dripping taps.

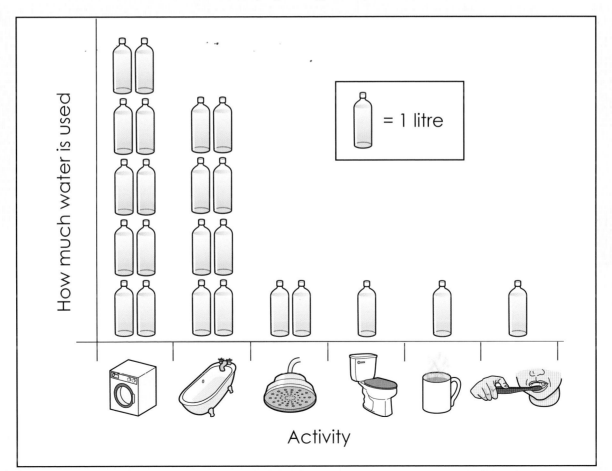

Using soil

Soil is the **material** that covers much of Earth. Soil is made up of tiny pieces of rock and clay. It is also made up of air and water mixed with pieces of dead plants and animals.

 Soil is full of living things. Earthworms, slugs, and beetles live in soil. These animals help to keep soil healthy.

Q What grows in soil?

CLUES

- What has roots under the ground?
- What grows fruits and seeds?

11

A Plants grow in soil.

Plants are useful in many different ways. Plants give us food such as fruit, vegetables, and nuts. Many other things that we use every day are made from plants.

Plants can be used to make:

➠ fabrics and clothes

➠ medicines

➠ herbs and spices

➠ cooking oil

➠ rubber.

The fruit and cereal in this bowl are plant products that we eat. The wooden handle of the spoon is also a plant product.

Using trees

Trees are plants that give us wood. They also give us fruit. Wood is used to make furniture such as chairs and tables. It is also used to build houses. Wood can also be used as a **fuel** for cooking and heating.

Q

What else can be made from trees?

?

CLUES

- What do you write on?
- What do you wrap presents in?
- What is a book made of?

15

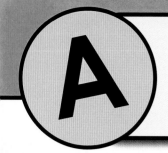

A

Wood can be used to make paper.

The wood is cut into small chips. Hot water is added to make the chips into a mushy **pulp**. The pulp is dried and pressed to make sheets of paper.

Paper can be used to make many different things, such as:

⟹ books

⟹ wrapping paper

⟹ paper bags

⟹ exercise books

⟹ newspapers and magazines.

Using fuels

Fuels can be used to make light and heat. Wood can be burned to make heat. Fuels are also used to make things work. Cars and other machines need fuel to make them work.

Q Which **solid** fuel comes from deep underground?

? CLUES

- This fuel is hard and black.
- This fuel can be burned to make heat.

19

A Coal is a fuel that is dug out of the ground.

Coal is made from plant **materials** that have been under the ground for millions of years. Coal is used to make a type of **energy** called **electricity**.

↑ Electricity is used to light and heat homes and offices.

Oil is another fuel that is found under the ground. It is also made from plant materials. It is a thick, dark liquid. Oil is used to make **petrol**. Petrol is used to make cars, planes, and other machines work.

→ An oil rig is where people work to get oil from under the ground. Oil rigs are built on land or in the sea.

Using rocks and metals

Rocks are hard, **solid** parts of Earth. Many rocks are cut out of the ground to use as **materials** for building.

Most metals are made of materials that are dug out of rocky ground. Gold, copper, and aluminium are all types of metal. Gold is used to make jewellery. Copper is used to make saucepans. Aluminium is used to make drinks cans.

 Can you name the materials used to make these objects?

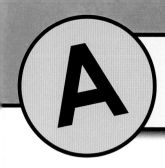

glass   paper   metal

Glass is made mainly from a special type of sand. Marbles are made of glass. Paper in books is made from wood. The watering can is made from metal.

24

All these materials can be used again to save resources. Metal and glass can be melted down and used to make new cans and bottles. Paper can be chopped up into **pulp** to make new paper. This is called **recycling**.

Saving resources

We are using resources such as **materials** and **fuels** very fast. We need to be careful how we use Earth's resources. **Recycling** is one way to save materials. All of these items can be recycled:

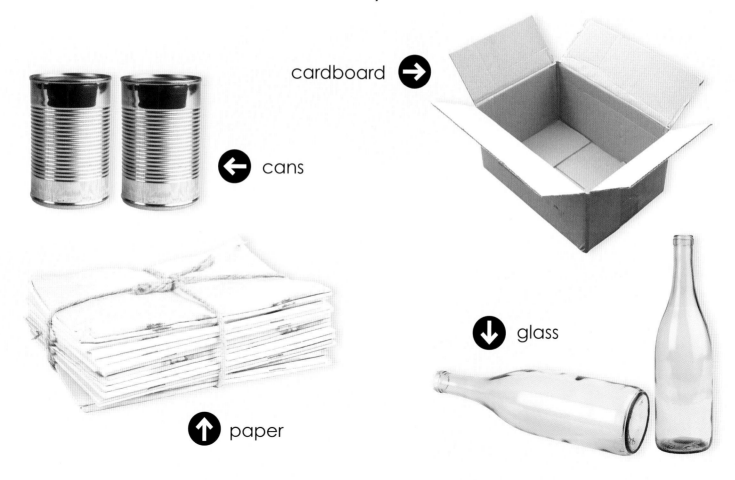

cardboard ➡

⬅ cans

⬇ glass

⬆ paper

We need to replace the things we take from Earth. For example, trees can be used for many things. Trees are also homes and food for many animals. When trees are cut down for fuel or materials, new trees should be planted.

We need to find ways to save Earth's resources. Water, wind, and solar power can be used to make light and heat. If we use these forms of energy we will not need to use so much **coal** and **oil**.

The power of the Sun can be used to make **electricity**.

28

We need to take care of Earth. Earth's resources are important for all living things. We need clean air and water. We need good soil to grow things. We need to use the Earth's resources carefully.

Checklist

Earth's resources are:

 air

 water

 soil

 materials

 fuels

Glossary

coal hard, black material dug from the ground in lumps

electricity form of energy that makes light and heat and can make machines work

energy something that gives power

fuel substance used to make heat or light, usually by being burned. Coal, gas, and oil are fuels.

materials something that we use to make other things. Clay is the material used to make pots.

oil thick, dark liquid found deep under the ground

petrol a type of fuel made from oil

pulp soft, wet mixture

recycling using something again or making it into something new

solid something which has a definite shape. Ice, wood, and stone are all solid.

Index